IN FLANDERS FIELDS

IN FLANDERS FIELDS

AND OTHER POEMS OF THE FIRST WORLD WAR

Edited by Brian Busby

ARCTURUS

For Corporal William H. Humphreys
Machine Gun Corps

This edition published in 2005 by Arcturus Publishing Limited
26/27 Bickels Yard, 151–153 Bermondsey Street,
London SE1 3HA

Published for
CHARTWELL BOOKS, INC.
A Division of
BOOK SALES, INC.
114 Northfield Avenue
Edison, New Jersey 08837

ISBN-13: 978-1-84193-346-7
ISBN-10 1-84193-346-5

Printed in China

CONTENTS

Introduction 6

Rupert Brooke 12

R. W. Sterling 18

W. S. S. Lyon 20

Colwyn Philipps 22

Julian Grenfell 24

Charles Hamilton Sorley 28

Cyril Horne 34

J. W. Streets 36

Alexander Robertson 37

W. N. Hodgson 38

Alan Seeger 45

Richard Dennys 59

Harold Beckh 63

T. M. Kettle 65

E. Wyndham Tennant 66

Leslie Coulson 76

Arthur Graeme West 87

Edward Thomas 95

J. M. Langstaff 104

Robert Ernest Vernède 105

Hamish (Arthur James) Mann 106

Harold Parry 110

Bernard Freeman Trotter 111

Francis Ledwidge 121

John McCrae 125

Horace Bray 131

Isaac Rosenberg 135

Henry Lamont Simpson 151

Joyce Kilmer 153

Wilfred Owen 157

Biographies 178

Index of Titles 189

Index of First Lines 191

INTRODUCTION

The poetry contained in this book was composed by men who died in the First World War. A few entered the conflict never having written verse. Many died without seeing their work in print. Most would, no doubt, have never considered themselves poets at all; yet that is how they are remembered nine decades later.

John McCrae, whose poem 'In Flanders Fields' lends its title to this book, holds a unique position amongst these poets; he entered the conflict as a war veteran, having served as a commissioned officer in the Boer War.

McCrae wrote only two poems during his second war, 'The Anxious Dead' and 'In

Flanders Fields', the latter becoming the best known, most enduring of the conflict. It is believed to have been inspired by the death of his friend Alexis Helmer. A Canadian lieutenant, Helmer was killed during the Second Battle of Ypres, the result of a direct hit by a German shell. His gathered remains were buried the same day, McCrae conducting a service at which he recited memorized passages from the Church of England's 'Order for the Burial of the Dead'.

The popularity of 'In Flanders Fields' brought greater attention to McCrae's poetry, particularly those few poems inspired by military life and death. One of these poems, 'The Unconquered Dead', is the only verse not written during the First World War included in this anthology.

A collection of McCrae's poetry, the only one, was published a year after his death. In this respect, McCrae is anything but unique amongst the war poets. Over seventy collections of English language poems, each the work of a single fallen soldier, appeared during the war and in the months that followed. They were published and, in all but a few cases, soon went out of print. For the most part, these are works of voices never again heard, except in collections such as this.

It was the 'War to End All Wars' and, although so very many wars have followed, the conflict remains unique for the great verse it inspired and the number of great poets it killed. Of course, not all the war poets died in the conflict. Siegfied Sassoon and Robert Graves served, survived, and continued to write for much of the twentieth century. Their impressive bodies of work raise the issue of what was lost to the realm of literature. What, one wonders, would have been Wilfred Owen's place in the post-war world? Speculation such as this is, without question, a fool's game, but one can't help but picture the poet as one of the century's great men of letters; indeed, it is difficult to imagine otherwise. Certainly the death of Isaac Rosenberg was a loss not only to poetry, but to the world of art. And what of the effect the war had on those who survived; men like Canada's W.W.E. Ross, who returned home forever transformed by the trenches, the shelling and the gas?

What follows is a long procession of voices silenced by the war, beginning with Rupert Brooke and R.W. Sterling, both of whom died on 23 April 1915. The union brought by the date of their respective deaths is in no way unusual; at least seven published poets,

W.N. Hodgson, J.W. Streets and Alexander Robertson among them, were killed on 1 July 1916, the first day of the Battle of the Somme. The cortège ends with Wilfred Owen, the war's greatest poet, killed by machine-gun fire just seven days before the end of the conflict. It is said that his parents received the news of his death to the sound of church bells ringing in celebration of the Armistice.

BRIAN BUSBY

April 2005

1914
I. Peace

Now, God be thanked Who has matched us with His hour,

And caught our youth, and wakened us from sleeping,

With hand made sure, clear eye, and sharpened power,

To turn, as swimmers into cleanness leaping,

Glad from a world grown old and cold and weary,

Leave the sick hearts that honour could not move,

And half-men, and their dirty songs and dreary,

And all the little emptiness of love!

Oh! we, who have known shame, we have found release there,

Where there's no ill, no grief, but sleep has mending,

Naught broken save this body, lost but breath;

Nothing to shake the laughing heart's long peace there

But only agony, and that has ending;

And the worst friend and enemy is but Death.

II. Safety

Dear! of all happy in the hour, most blest

He who has found our hid security,

Assured in the dark tides of the world at rest,

And heard our word, 'Who is so safe as we?'

We have found safety with all things undying,

The winds, and morning, tears of men and mirth,

The deep night, and birds singing, and clouds flying,

And sleep, and freedom, and the autumnal earth.

We have built a house that is not for Time's throwing.

We have gained a peace unshaken by pain for ever.

War knows no power. Safe shall be my going,

Secretly armed against all death's endeavour;

Safe though all safety's lost; safe where men fall;

And if these poor limbs die, safest of all.

III. The Dead

Blow out, you bugles, over the rich Dead!
There's none of these so lonely and poor of old,
But, dying, has made us rarer gifts than gold.
These laid the world away; poured out the red
Sweet wine of youth; gave up the years to be
Of work and joy, and that unhoped serene,
That men call age; and those who would have been,
Their sons, they gave, their immortality.

Blow, bugles, blow! They brought us, for our dearth,
Holiness, lacked so long, and Love, and Pain.
Honour has come back, as a king, to earth,
And paid his subjects with a royal wage;
And nobleness walks in our ways again;
And we have come into our heritage.

IV. The Dead

These hearts were woven of human joys and cares,

Washed marvellously with sorrow, swift to mirth.

The years had given them kindness. Dawn was theirs,

And sunset, and the colours of the earth.

These had seen movement, and heard music; known

Slumber and waking; loved; gone proudly friended;

Felt the quick stir of wonder; sat alone;

Touched flowers and furs and cheeks. All this is ended.

There are waters blown by changing winds to laughter

And lit by the rich skies, all day. And after,

Frost, with a gesture, stays the waves that dance

And wandering loveliness. He leaves a white

Unbroken glory, a gathered radiance,

A width, a shining peace, under the night.

V. The Soldier

If I should die, think only this of me:
That there's some corner of a foreign field
That is for ever England. There shall be
In that rich earth a richer dust concealed;
A dust whom England bore, shaped, made aware,
Gave, once, her flowers to love, her ways to roam,
A body of England's, breathing English air,
Washed by the rivers, blest by suns of home.

And think, this heart, all evil shed away,
A pulse in the eternal mind, no less
Gives somewhere back the thoughts by England given;
Her sights and sounds; dreams happy as her day;
And laughter, learnt of friends; and gentleness,
In hearts at peace, under an English heaven.

RUPERT BROOKE

Last Lines

I

Ah! Hate like this would freeze our human tears,

And stab the morning star:

Not it, not it commands and mourns and bears

The storm and bitter glory of red war.

II

To J.H.S.M., killed in action, March 13, 1915

O brother, I have sung no dirge for thee:

Nor for all time to come

Can song reveal my grief's infinity:

The menace of thy silence made me dumb.

R. W. STERLING

I Tracked a Dead Man
Down a Trench

I tracked a dead man down a trench,
  I knew not he was dead.
They told me he had gone that way,
  And there his foot-marks led

The trench was long and close and curved,
  It seemed without an end;
And as I threaded each new bay
  I thought to see my friend.

I went there stooping to the ground,
  For, should I raise my head,
Death watched to spring; and how should then
  A dead man find the dead?

At last I saw his back. He crouched
As still as still could be,
And when I called his name aloud
He did not answer me.

The floor-way of the trench was wet
Where he was crouching dead:
The water of the pool was brown,
And round him it was red.

I stole up softly where he stayed
With head hung down all slack,
And on his shoulders laid my hands
And drew him gently back.

And then, as I had guessed, I saw
His head, and how the crown –
I saw then why he crouched so still,
And why his head hung down.

W. S. S. LYON

Release

There is a healing magic in the night,

The breeze blows cleaner than it did by day,

Forgot the fever of the fuller light,

And sorrow sinks insensibly away

As if some saint a cool white hand did lay

Upon the brow, and calm the restless brain.

The moon looks down with pale unpassioned ray –

Sufficient for the hour is its pain.

Be still and feel the night that hides away earth's stain.

Be still and loose the sense of God in you,

Be still and send your soul into the all,

The vasty distance where the stars shine blue,

No longer antlike on the earth to crawl.

Released from time and sense of great or small,

Float on the pinions of the Night-Queen's wings;

Soar till the swift inevitable fall

Will drag you back into all the world's small things;

Yet for an hour be one with all escaped things.

COLWYN PHILIPPS

Into Battle

(Flanders, April 1915)

The naked earth is warm with Spring,
And with green grass and bursting trees
Leans to the sun's gaze glorying,
And quivers in the sunny breeze;

And life is colour and warmth and light,
And a striving evermore for these;
And he is dead who will not fight;
And who dies fighting has increase.

The fighting man shall from the sun
Take warmth, and life from the glowing earth;
Speed with the light-foot winds to run,

BRUSH, ERIN RACHEL
78370
Unclaim : 2/26/2022

Held date   : 2/17/2022
Pickup location : Garden Home Community Library

Title   : In Flanders fields : and other
 poems of the First World War
Call number   : 821 IN
Item barcode   : 33614035193563
Assigned branch : Cedar Mill Library

Notes:

And with the trees to newer birth;
And find, when fighting shall be done,
Great rest, and fullness after dearth.

All the bright company of Heaven
Hold him in their high comradeship,
The Dog-Star, and the Sisters Seven,
Orion's Belt and sworded hip.

The woodland trees that stand together,
They stand to him each one a friend;
They gently speak in the windy weather;
They guide to valley and ridge's end.

The kestrel hovering by day,
And the little owls that call by night,
Bid him be swift and keen as they,
As keen of ear, as swift of sight.

The blackbird sings to him, 'Brother, brother,
If this be the last song you shall sing,
Sing well, for you may not sing another;
Brother, sing.'

In dreary, doubtful, waiting hours,
Before the brazen frenzy starts,
The horses show him nobler powers;
O patient eyes, courageous hearts!

And when the burning moment breaks,
And all things else are out of mind,
And only joy of battle takes
Him by the throat, and makes him blind,

Through joy and blindness he shall know,
Not caring much to know, that still
Nor lead nor steel shall reach him, so
That it be not the Destined Will.

The thundering line of battle stands,
And in the air death moans and sings;
But Day shall clasp him with strong hands,
And Night shall fold him in soft wings.

JULIAN GRENFELL

To Germany

You are blind like us. Your hurt no man designed,
And no man claimed the conquest of your land.
But gropers both, through fields of thought confined,
We stumble and we do not understand.
You only saw your future bigly planned,
And we the tapering paths of our own mind,
And in each other's dearest ways we stand,
And hiss and hate. And the blind fight the blind.

When it is peace, then we may view again
With new-won eyes each other's truer form,
And wonder. Grown more loving-kind and warm
We'll grasp firm hands and laugh at the old pain,
When it is peace. But until peace, the storm,
The darkness and the thunder and the rain.

CHARLES HAMILTON SORLEY

All the Hills and Vales Along

All the hills and vales along
Earth is bursting into song,
And the singers are the chaps
Who are going to die perhaps.
O sing, marching men,
Till the valleys ring again.
Give your gladness to earth's keeping,
So be glad, when you are sleeping.

Cast away regret and rue,
Think what you are marching to.
Little live, great pass.
Jesus Christ and Barabbas
Were found the same day.
This died, that went his way.
So sing with joyful breath,

For why, you are going to death.
Teeming earth will surely store
All the gladness that you pour.

Earth that never doubts nor fears,
Earth that knows of death, not tears,
Earth that bore with joyful ease
Hemlock for Socrates,
Earth that blossomed and was glad
'Neath the cross that Christ had,
Shall rejoice and blossom too
When the bullet reaches you.
Wherefore, men marching
On the road to death, sing!
Pour your gladness on earth's head,
So be merry, so be dead.

From the hills and valleys earth

Shouts back the sound of mirth,

Tramp of feet and lilt of song

Ringing all the road along.

All the music of their going,

Ringing swinging glad song-throwing,

Earth will echo still, when foot

Lies numb and voice mute.

On, marching men, on

To the gates of death with song.

Sow your gladness for earth's reaping,

So you may be glad, though sleeping.

Strew your gladness on earth's bed,

So be merry, so be dead.

CHARLES HAMILTON SORLEY

When You See Millions of the Mouthless Dead

When you see millions of the mouthless dead
Across your dreams in pale battalions go,
Say not soft things as other men have said,
That you'll remember. For you need not so.
Give them not praise. For, deaf, how should they know
It is not curses heaped on each gashed head?
Nor tears. Their blind eyes see not your tears flow.
Nor honour. It is easy to be dead.
Say only this, 'They are dead.' Then add thereto,
'Yet many a better one has died before.'
Then, scanning all the o'ercrowded mass, should you
Perceive one face that you loved heretofore,
It is a spook. None wears the face you knew.
Great death has made all his for evermore.

CHARLES HAMILTON SORLEY

from *Dolores*

Six of us lay in a Dugout
At ease, with our limbs astretch,
And worshipped a feminine picture
Cut from a week-old 'Sketch'.
We gazed at her Silken Stockings,
We studied her Cupid bow,
And we thought of the Suppers we used to buy
And the girls we used to know.
And we all, in our several fashions,
Paid toll to the Lady's charms,

From the man of a hundred passions

To the Subaltern child-in-arms.

Never the sketch of a master

So jealously kept and prized,

Never a woman of flesh and blood

So truly idealized.

And because of her slender ankle,

And her coiffure – distinctly French –

We called her 'La Belle Dolores' –

'The Vivandière of the Trench.'

CYRIL HORNE

Love of Life

Reach out thy hands, thy spirit's hands, to me

And pluck the youth, the magic from my heart –

Magic of dreams whose sensibility

Is plumed like the light; visions that start

Mad pressure in the blood; desire that thrills

The soul with mad delight: to yearning wed

All slothfulness of life; draw from its bed

The soul of dawn across the twilight hills.

Reach out thy hands, O spirit, till I feel

That I am fully thine; for I shall live

In the proud consciousness that thou dost give,

And if thy twilight fingers round me steal

And draw me unto death – thy votary

Am I, O Life; reach out thy hands to me!

J.W. STREETS

Lines Before Going

Soon is the night of our faring to regions unknown,

There not to flinch at the challenge suddenly thrown

By the great process of Being – daily to see

The utmost that life has of horror, and yet to be

Calm and the masters of fear. Aware that the soul

Lives as a part and alone for the weal of the whole,

So shall the mind be free from the pain of regret,

Vain and enfeebling, firm in each venture, and yet

Brave not as those who despair, but keen to maintain,

Though not assured, hope in beneficent pain.

Hope that the truth of the world is not what appears,

Hope in the triumph of man for the price of his tears.

ALEXANDER ROBERTSON

Ave, Mater — atque Vale

The deathless mother, grey and battle-scarred,
Lies in the sanctuary of stately trees,
Where the deep Northern night is saffron starred
Above her head, and thro' the dusk she sees
God's shadowy fortress keep unsleeping guard.

From her full breast we drank of joy and mirth
And gave to her a boy's unreasoned heart,
Wherein Time's fullness was to bring to birth
Such passionate allegiance that to part
Seemed like the passing of all light on earth.

Now on the threshold of a man's estate,
With a new depth of love akin to pain
I ask thy blessing, while I dedicate

My life and sword, with promise to maintain
Thine ancient honour yet inviolate.

Last night dream-hearted in the Abbey's spell
We stood to sing old Simeon's passing hymn,
When sudden splendour of the sunset fell
Full on my eyes, and passed and left all dim –
At once a summons and a deep farewell.

I am content – our life is but a trust
From the great hand of God, and if I keep
The immortal Treasure clean of mortal rust
Against His claim, 'tis well and let me sleep
Among the not dishonourable dust.

W.N. HODGSON

Release

A leaping wind from England,
The skies without a stain,
Clean cut against the morning
Slim poplars after rain,
The foolish noise of sparrows
And starlings in a wood –
After the grime of battle
We know that these are good.

Death whining down from heaven,
Death roaring from the ground,
Death stinking in the nostril,
Death shrill in every sound,

Doubting we charged and conquered –
Hopeless we struck and stood;
Now when the fight is ended
We know that it was good.

We that have seen the strongest
Cry like a beaten child,
The sanest eyes unholy,
The cleanest hands defiled,
We that have known the heart-blood
Less than the lees of wine,
We that have seen men broken,
We know that man is divine.

W.N. HODGSON

Before Action

By all the glories of the day
And the cool evening's benison,
By that last sunset touch that lay
Upon the hills when day was done,
By beauty lavishly outpoured
And blessings carelessly received,
By all the days that I have lived
Make me a soldier, Lord.

By all of man's hopes and fears,
And all the wonders poets sing,
The laughter of unclouded years,
And every sad and lovely thing;
By the romantic ages stored
With high endeavour that was his,
By all his mad catastrophes
Make me a man, O Lord.

I, that on my unfamiliar hill

Saw with uncomprehending eyes

A hundred of Thy sunsets spill

Their fresh and sanguine sacrifice,

Ere the sun swings his noonday sword

Must say good-bye to all of this; –

By all delights that I shall miss,

Help me to die, O Lord.

W.N. HODGSON

Resurgam

Exiled afar from youth and happy love,

If Death should ravish my fond spirit hence

I have no doubt but, like a homing dove,

It would return to its dear residence,

And through a thousand stars find out the road

Back into earthly flesh that was its loved abode.

ALAN SEEGER

The Aisne, 1914–15

We first saw fire on the tragic slopes
Where the flood-tide of France's early gain,
Big with wrecked promise and abandoned hopes,
Broke in a surf of blood along the Aisne.

The charge her heroes left us, we assumed,
What, dying, they reconquered, we preserved,
In the chill trenches, harried, shelled, entombed,
Winter came down on us, but no man swerved.

Winter came down on us. The low clouds, torn
In the stark branches of the riven pines,
Blurred the white rockets that from dusk till morn
Traced the wide curve of the close-grappling lines.

In rain, and fog that on the withered hill
Froze before dawn, the lurking foe drew down;
Or light snows fell that made forlorner still
The ravaged country and the ruined town;

Or the long clouds would end. Intensely fair,
The winter constellations blazing forth –
Perseus, the Twins, Orion, the Great Bear –
Gleamed on our bayonets pointing to the north.

And the lone sentinel would start and soar
On wings of strong emotion as he knew
That kinship with the stars that only War
Is great enough to lift man's spirit to.

And ever down the curving front, aglow
With the pale rockets' intermittent light,
He heard, like distant thunder, growl and grow
The rumble of far battles in the night, –

Rumors, reverberant indistinct, remote,
Borne from red fields whose martial names have won
The power to thrill like a far trumpet-note, –
Vic, Vailly, Soupir, Hurtelise, Craonne ...

Craonne, before thy cannon-swept plateau,
Where like sere leaves lay strewn September's dead,
I found for all dear things I forfeited
A recompense I would not now forego.

For that high fellowship was ours then
With those who, championing another's good,
More than dull Peace or its poor votaries could,
Taught us the dignity of being men.

There we drained deeper the deep cup of life,
And on sublimer summits came to learn,
After soft things, the terrible and stern,
After sweet Love, the majesty of Strife;

There where we faced under those frowning heights
The blast that maims, the hurricane that kills;
There where the watchlights on the winter hills
Flickered like balefire through inclement nights;

There where, firm links in the unyielding chain,
Where fell the long-planned blow and fell in vain –
Hearts worthy of the honor and the trial,
We helped to hold the lines along the Aisne.

ALAN SEEGER

Champagne, 1914–15

In the glad revels, in the happy fetes,
When cheeks are flushed, and glasses gilt and pearled
With the sweet wine of France that concentrates
The sunshine and the beauty of the world,

Drink sometimes, you whose footsteps yet may tread
The undisturbed, delightful paths of Earth,
To those whose blood, in pious duty shed,
Hallows the soil where that same wine had birth.

Here, by devoted comrades laid away,
Along our lines they slumber where they fell,
Beside the crater at the Ferme d'Alger
And up the bloody slopes of La Pompelle,

And round the city whose cathedral towers

The enemies of Beauty dared profane,

And in the mat of multicolored flowers

That clothe the sunny chalk-fields of Champagne.

Under the little crosses where they rise

The soldier rests. Now round him undismayed

The cannon thunders, and at night he lies

At peace beneath the eternal fusillade. ...

That other generations might possess –

From shame and menace free in years to come –

A richer heritage of happiness,

He marched to that heroic martyrdom.

Esteeming less the forfeit that he paid

Than undishonored that his flag might float

Over the towers of liberty, he made

His breast the bulwark and his blood the moat.

Obscurely sacrificed, his nameless tomb,
Bare of the sculptor's art, the poet's lines,
Summer shall flush with poppy-fields in bloom,
And Autumn yellow with maturing vines.

There the grape-pickers at their harvesting
Shall lightly tread and load their wicker trays,
Blessing his memory as they toil and sing
In the slant sunshine of October days. ...

I love to think that if my blood should be
So privileged to sink where his has sunk,
I shall not pass from Earth entirely,
But when the banquet rings, when healths are drunk,

And faces that the joys of living fill
Glow radiant with laughter and good cheer,
In beaming cups some spark of me shall still
Brim toward the lips that once I held so dear.

So shall one coveting no higher plane
Than nature clothes in color and flesh and tone,
Even from the grave put upward to attain
The dreams youth cherished and missed and might have known;

And that strong need that strove unsatisfied
Toward earthly beauty in all forms it wore,
Not death itself shall utterly divide
From the belovèd shapes it thirsted for.

Alas, how many an adept for whose arms
Life held delicious offerings perished here,
How many in the prime of all that charms,
Crowned with all gifts that conquer and endear!

Honor them not so much with tears and flowers,
But you with whom the sweet fulfilment lies,
Where in the anguish of atrocious hours
Turned their last thoughts and closed their dying eyes,

Rather when music on bright gatherings lays
Its tender spell, and joy is uppermost,
Be mindful of the men they were, and raise
Your glasses to them in one silent toast.

Drink to them – amorous of dear Earth as well,
They asked no tribute lovelier than this –
And in the wine that ripened where they fell,
Oh, frame your lips as though it were a kiss.

ALAN SEEGER

I Have a Rendezvous with Death

I have a rendezvous with Death
At some disputed barricade,
When Spring comes back with rustling shade
And apple-blossoms fill the air –
I have a rendezvous with Death
When Spring brings back blue days and fair.

It may be he shall take my hand
And lead me into his dark land
And close my eyes and quench my breath –
It may be I shall pass him still.
I have a rendezvous with Death
On some scarred slope of battered hill,
When Spring comes round again this year
And the first meadow-flowers appear.

God knows 'twere better to be deep
Pillowed in silk and scented down,
Where love throbs out in blissful sleep,
Pulse nigh to pulse, and breath to breath,
Where hushed awakenings are dear...
But I've a rendezvous with Death
At midnight in some flaming town,
When Spring trips north again this year,
And I to my pledged word am true,
I shall not fail that rendezvous.

ALAN SEEGER

War

To end the dreary day,

The sun brought fire

And smote the grey

Of the heavens away

In his desire

That the evening sky might glow as red

As showed the earth with blood and ire.

The distant cannon's boom

In a land oppressed

Still spake the gloom

Of a country's doom,

Denying rest.

'War!' – called the frightened rooks and flew

From the crimson East to the crimson West.

Then, lest the dark might mar

The sky o'erhead,

There shone a star,

In the night afar

O'er each man's bed,

A symbol of undying peace,

The peace encompassing the dead.

RICHARD DENNYS

Better Far to Pass Away

Better far to pass away

While the limbs are strong and young,

Ere the ending of the day,

Ere youth's lusty song be sung.

Hot blood pulsing through the veins,

Youth's high hope a burning fire,
Young men needs must break the chains
That hold them from their hearts' desire.

My friends the hills, the sea, the sun,
The winds, the woods, the clouds, the trees –
How feebly, if my youth were done,
Could I, an old man, relish these!
With laughter, then, I'll go to greet
What Fate has still in store for me,
And welcome Death if we should meet,
And bear him willing company.

My share of fourscore years and ten
I'll gladly yield to any man,
And take no thought of 'where' or 'when,'
Contented with my shorter span,
For I have learned what love may be,
And found a heart that understands,

And known a comrade's constancy,
And felt the grip of friendly hands.

Come when it may, the stern decree
For me to leave the cheery throng
And quit the sturdy company
Of brothers that I work among.
No need for me to look askance,
Since no regret my prospect mars.
My day was happy – and perchance
The coming night is full of stars.

RICHARD DENNYS

The Song of Sheffield

Shells, shells, shells!

The song of the city of steel;

Hammer and turn, and file,

Furnace, and lathe, and wheel.

Tireless machinery,

Man's ingenuity,

Making a way for the martial devil's meal.

Shells, shells, shells!

Out of the furnace blaze;

Roll, roll, roll,

Into the workshop's maze.

Ruthless machinery

Boring eternally,

Boring a hole for the shattering charge that stays.

Shells, shells, shells!

The song of the city of steel;

List to the devils' mirth,

Hark to their laughters' peal:

Sheffield's machinery

Crushing humanity

Neath devil-ridden death's impassive heel.

HAROLD BECKH

To My Daughter Betty,
The Gift of God

In wiser days, my darling rosebud, blown
To beauty proud as was your mother's prime,
In that desired, delayed, incredible time,
You'll ask why I abandoned you, my own,
And the dear heart that was your baby throne,
To dice with death. And oh! they'll give you rhyme
And reason: some will call the thing sublime,

And some decry it in a knowing tone.
So here, while the mad guns curse overhead,
And tired men sigh with mud for couch and floor,
Know that we fools, now with the foolish dead,
Died not for flag, nor King, nor Emperor, –
But for a dream, born in a herdsman's shed,
And for the secret Scripture of the poor.

T.M. KETTLE

Light After Darkness

Once more the Night, like some great dark drop-scene
Eclipsing horrors for a brief *entr'acte*,
Descends, lead-weighty. Now the space between,
Fringed with the eager eyes of men, is racked
By spark-tailed lights, curvetting far and high,
Swift smoke-flecked coursers, raking the black sky.

And as each sinks in ashes grey, one more
Rises to fall, and so through all the hours
They strive like petty empires by the score,
Each confident of its success and powers,
And, hovering at its zenith, each will show
Pale, rigid faces, lying dead, below.

There shall they lie, tainting the innocent air,

Until the dawn, deep veiled in mournful grey,

Sadly and quietly shall lay them bare,

The broken heralds of a doleful day.

E. WYNDHAM TENNANT

Home Thoughts from Laventie

Green gardens in Laventie!

Soldiers only know the street

Where the mud is churned and splashed about

By battle-wending feet;

And yet beside one stricken house there is a glimpse of grass, –

Look for it when you pass.

Beyond the church whose pitted spire

Seems balanced on a strand

Of swaying stone and tottering brick,

Two roofless ruins stand;

And here, among the wreckage, where the back-wall should have been,

We found a garden green.

The grass was never trodden on,

The little path of gravel

Was overgrown with celandine;

No other folk did travel

Along its weedy surface but the nimble-footed mouse,

Running from house to house.

So all along the tender blades

Of soft and vivid grass

We lay, nor heard the limber wheels

That pass and ever pass

In noisy continuity until their stony rattle

Seems in itself a battle.

At length we rose up from this ease

Of tranquil happy mind,

And searched the garden's little length

Some new pleasaunce to find;

And there some yellow daffodils, and jasmine hanging high,

Did rest the tired eye.

The fairest and most fragrant

Of the many sweets we found

Was a little bush of Daphne flower

Upon a mossy mound,

And so thick were the blossoms set and so divine the scent,

That we were well content.

Hungry for Spring I bent my head,

The perfume fanned my face,

And all my soul was dancing

In that lovely little place,

Dancing with a measured step from wrecked and shattered towns

Away ... upon the Downs.

I saw green banks of daffodil,

Slim poplars in the breeze,

Great tan-brown hares in gusty March

A-courting on the leas.

And meadows, with their glittering streams – and silver-scurrying dace –

Home, what a perfect place!

E. WYNDHAM TENNANT

The Mad Soldier

I dropp'd here three weeks ago, yes – I know,
And it's bitter cold at night, since the fight –
I could tell you if I chose – no one knows
Excep' me and four or five, what ain't alive
I can see them all asleep, three men deep,
And they're nowhere near a fire – but our wire
Has 'em fast as fast can be. Can't you see
When the flare goes up? Ssh! boys; what's that noise?
Do you know what these rats eat? Body-meat!
After you've been down a week, an' your cheek
Gets as pale as life, and night seems as white
As the day, only the rats and their brats
Seem more hungry when the day's gone away –
An' they look as big as bulls, an' they pulls
Till you almost sort o' shout – but the drought
What you hadn't felt before makes you sore.

And at times you even think of a drink ...

There's a leg across my thighs – if my eyes

Weren't too sore, I'd like to see who it be,

Wonder if I'd know the bloke if I woke? –

Woke? By damn, I'm not asleep – there's a heap

Of us wond'ring why the hell we're not well ...

Leastways I am – since I came it's the same

With the others – they don't know what *I* do,

Or they wouldn't gape and grin. – It's a sin

To say that Hell is hot – 'cause it's not:

Mind you, I know very well we're in hell. –

– In a twisted hump we lie – heaping high

Yes! an' higher every day. – Oh, I say,

This chap's heavy on my thighs – damn his eyes.

E. WYNDHAM TENNANT

Reincarnation

I too remember distant golden days
When even my soul was young; I see the sand
Whirl in a blinding pillar towards the band
Of orange sky-line 'neath a turquoise blaze –
(Some burnt-out sky spread o'er a glistening land)
– And slim brown jargoning men in blue and gold,
I know it all so well, I understand
The ecstasy of worship ages-old.

Hear the first truth: The great far-seeing soul
Is ever in the humblest husk; I see
How each succeeding section takes its toll
In fading cycles of old memory.
And each new life the next life shall control
Until perfection reach eternity.

E. WYNDHAM TENNANT

From an Outpost

I've tramped South England up and down
    Down Dorset way, down Devon way,
    Through every little ancient town
    Down Dorset way, down Devon way.
    I mind the old stone churches there,
    The taverns round the market square,
    The cobbled streets, the garden flowers,
    The sundials telling peaceful hours
    Down Dorset way, down Devon way.

    The Meadowlands are green and fair
    Down Somerset and Sussex way,
    The clover scent is in the air
    Down Somerset and Sussex way.

I mind the deep-thatched homesteads there
The noble downlands, clean and bare.
The sheepfolds and the cattle byres,
The blue wood-smoke from shepherds' fires
Down Dorset way, down Devon way,

Mayhap I shall not walk again
Down Dorset way, down Devon way,
Nor pick a posy in a lane
Down Somerset and Sussex way.
But though my bones, unshriven, rot
In some far distant alien spot,
What soul I have shall rest from care
To know that meadows still are fair
Down Dorset way, down Devon way.

LESLIE COULSON

The Rainbow

I watch the white dawn gleam,

To the thunder of hidden guns.

I hear the hot shells scream

Through skies as sweet as a dream

Where the silver dawn-break runs.

And stabbing of light

Scorches the virginal white.

But I feel in my being the old, high, sanctified thrill,

And I thank the gods that dawn is beautiful still.

From death that hurtles by

I crouch in the trench day-long

But up to a cloudless sky

From the ground where our dead men lie

A brown lark soars in song.

Through the tortured air,

Rent by the shrapnel's flare,

Over the troubleless dead he carols his fill,

And I thank the gods that the birds are beautiful still.

Where the parapet is low

And level with the eye

Poppies and cornflowers glow

And the corn sways to and fro

In a pattern against the sky.

The gold stalks hide

Bodies of men who died

Charging at dawn through the dew to be killed or to kill.

I thank the gods that the flowers are beautiful still.

When night falls dark we creep

In silence to our dead.

We dig a few feet deep

And leave them there to sleep –

But blood at night is red,

Yea, even at night,

And a dead man's face is white.

And I dry my hands, that are also trained to kill,

And I look at the stars – for the stars are beautiful still.

LESLIE COULSON

'– But a Short Time to Live'

Our little hour – how swift it flies

When poppies flare and lilies smile;

How soon the fleeting minute dies,

Leaving us but a little while

To dream our dreams, to sing our song,

To pick the fruit, to pluck the flower,

The Gods – They do not give us long, –

One little hour.

Our little hour – how short it is

When Love with dew-eyed loveliness

Raises her lips for ours to kiss

And dies within our first caress.

Youth flickers out like wind-blown flame,

Sweets of to-day to-morrow sour,

For Time and Death, relentless, claim

Our little hour.

Our little hour – how short a time
To wage our wars, to fan our hates,
To take our fill of armoured crime,
To troop our banner, storm the gates.
Blood on the sword, our eyes blood-red,
Blind in our puny reign of power,
Do we forget how soon is sped
Our little hour.

Our little hour – how soon it dies;
How short a time to tell our beads,
To chant our feeble Litanies,
To think sweet thoughts, to do good deeds.
The altar lights grow pale and dim,
The bells hang silent in the tower –
So passes with the dying hymn
Our little hour.

LESLIE COULSON

Who Made the Law?

Who made the Law that men should die in meadows?
Who spake the word that blood should splash in lanes?
Who gave it forth that gardens should be bone-yards?
Who spread the hills with flesh, and blood, and brains?
Who made the Law?

Who made the Law that Death should stalk the village?
Who spake the word to kill among the sheaves,
Who gave it forth that death should lurk in hedgerows,
Who flung the dead among the fallen leaves?
Who made the Law?

Those who return shall find that peace endures,
Find old things old, and know the things they knew,
Walk in the garden, slumber by the fireside,
Share the peace of dawn, and dream amid the dew –
Those who return.

Those who return shall till the ancient pastures,
Clean-hearted men shall guide the plough-horse reins,
Some shall grow apples and flowers in the valleys,
Some shall go courting in summer down the lanes –
THOSE WHO RETURN.

But who made the Law? the Trees shall whisper to him:

'See, see the blood – the splashes on our bark!'

Walking the meadows, he shall hear bones crackle,

And fleshless mouths shall gibber in silent lanes at dark.

Who made the Law?

Who made the Law? At noon upon the hillside

His ears shall hear a moan, his cheeks shall feel a breath,

And all along the valleys, past gardens, croft, and homesteads,

He who made the Law,

HE who made the Law,

HE who made the Law shall walk along with Death.

WHO made the Law?

LESLIE COULSON

The Night Patrol

Over the top! The wire's thin here, unbarbed
Plain rusty coils, not staked, and low enough:
Full of old tins, though – 'When you're through, all three,
Aim quarter left for fifty yards or so,
Then straight for that new piece of German wire;
See if it's thick, and listen for a while
For sounds of working; don't run any risks;
About an hour; now, over!'
And we placed
Our hands on the topmost sand-bags, leapt, and stood
A second with curved backs, then crept to the wire,
Wormed ourselves tinkling through, glanced back, and dropped.
The sodden ground was splashed with shallow pools,
And tufts of crackling cornstalks, two years old,
No man had reaped, and patches of spring grass,

Half-seen, as rose and sank the flares, were strewn

The wrecks of our attack: the bandoliers,

Packs, rifles, bayonets, belts, and haversacks,

Shell fragments, and the huge whole forms of shells

Shot fruitlessly – and everywhere the dead.

Only the dead were always present – present

As a vile sickly smell of rottenness;

The rustling stubble and the early grass,

The slimy pools – the dead men stank through all,

Pungent and sharp; as bodies loomed before,

And as we passed, they stank: then dulled away

To that vague fœtor, all encompassing,

Infecting earth and air. They lay, all clothed,

Each in some new and piteous attitude

That we well marked to guide us back: as he,

Outside our wire, that lay on his back and crossed

His legs Crusader-wise; I smiled at that,

And thought on Elia and his Temple Church.

From him, at quarter left, lay a small corpse,

Down in a hollow, huddled as in a bed,

That one of us put his hand on unawares.

Next was a bunch of half a dozen men

All blown to bits, an archipelago

Of corrupt fragments, vexing to us three,

Who had no light to see by, save the flares.

On such a trail, so lit, for ninety yards

We crawled on belly and elbows, till we saw,

Instead of lumpish dead before our eyes,

The stakes and crosslines of the German wire.

We lay in shelter of the last dead man,

Ourselves as dead, and heard their shovels ring

Turning the earth, then talk and cough at times.

A sentry fired and a machine-gun spat;

They shot a glare above us, when it fell

And spluttered out in the pools of No Man's Land,

We turned and crawled past the remembered dead:

Past him and him, and them and him, until,

For he lay some way apart, we caught the scent

Of the Crusader and slid past his legs,

And through the wire and home, and got our rum.

ARTHUR GRAEME WEST

God! How I Hate You, You Young Cheerful Men

God! How I hate you, you young cheerful men,

Whose pious poetry blossoms on your graves

As soon as you are in them, nurtured up

By the salt of your corruption, and the tears

Of mothers, local vicars, college deans,

And flanked by prefaces and photographs

From all your minor poet friends – the fools –

Who paint their sentimental elegies

Where sure, no angel treads; and, living, share

The dead's brief immortality.

Oh Christ!

To think that one could spread the ductile wax

Of his fluid youth to Oxford's glowing fires

And take her seal so ill! Hark how one chants –

'Oh happy to have lived these epic days' –

'These epic days'! And *he'd* been to France,

And seen the trenches, glimpsed the huddled dead

In the periscope, hung in the rusting wire:

Choked by their sickly fœtor, day and night

Blown down his throat: stumbled through ruined hearths,

Proved all that muddy brown monotony,

Where blood's the only coloured thing. Perhaps

Had seen a man killed, a sentry shot at night,

Hunched as he fell, his feet on the firing-step,

His neck against the back slope of the trench,

Smashed like an egg-shell, and the warm grey brain
Spattered all bloody on the parados:
Had flashed a torch on his face, and known his friend,
Shot, breathing hardly, in ten minutes – gone!
Yet still God's in His heaven, all is right
In the best possible of worlds. The woe,
Even His scaled eyes *must* see, is partial, only
A seeming woe, we cannot understand.
God loves us, God looks down on this our strife
And smiles in pity, blows a pipe at times
And calls some warriors home. We do not die,
God would not let us, He is too 'intense',
Too 'passionate', a whole day sorrows He
Because a grass-blade dies. How rare life is!
On earth, the love and fellowship of men,
Men sternly banded: banded for what end?
Banded to maim and kill their fellow men –
For even Huns are men. In heaven above
A genial umpire, a good judge of sport,

Won't let us hurt each other! Let's rejoice
God keeps us faithful, pens us still in fold.
Ah, what a faith is ours (almost, it seems,
Large as a mustard-seed) – we trust and trust,
Nothing can shake us! Ah, how good God is
To suffer us to be born just now, when youth
That else would rust, can slake his blade in gore,
Where very God Himself does seem to walk
The bloody fields of Flanders He so loves!

ARTHUR GRAEME WEST

In Memoriam (Easter, 1915)

The flowers left thick at nightfall in the wood
This Eastertide call into mind the men,
Now far from home, who, with their sweethearts, should
Have gathered them and will do never again.

EDWARD THOMAS

Gone, Gone Again

Gone, gone again,
May, June, July,
And August gone,
Again gone by,

Not memorable

Save that I saw them go,

As past the empty quays

The rivers flow.

And now again,

In the harvest rain,

The Blenheim oranges

Fall grubby from the trees

As when I was young –

And when the lost one was here –

And when the war began

To turn young men to dung.

Look at the old house,

Outmoded, dignified,

Dark and untenanted,
With grass growing instead

Of the footsteps of life,
The friendliness, the strife;
In its beds have lain
Youth, love, age, and pain:

I am something like that;
Only I am not dead,
Still breathing and interested
In the house that is not dark: –

I am something like that:
Not one pane to reflect the sun,
For the schoolboys to throw at –
They have broken every one.

EDWARD THOMAS

Rain

Rain, midnight rain, nothing but the wild rain
On this bleak hut, and solitude, and me
Remembering again that I shall die
And neither hear the rain nor give it thanks
For washing me cleaner than I have been
Since I was born into this solitude.
Blessed are the dead that the rain rains upon:
But here I pray that none whom once I loved
Is dying to-night or lying still awake
Solitary, listening to the rain,
Either in pain or thus in sympathy
Helpless among the living and the dead,
Like a cold water among broken reeds,
Myriads of broken reeds all still and stiff,
Like me who have no love which this wild rain

Has not dissolved except the love of death,
If love it be for what is perfect and
Cannot, the tempest tells me, disappoint.

EDWARD THOMAS

The Cherry Trees

The cherry trees bend over and are shedding,
On the old road where all that passed are dead,
Their petals, strewing the grass as for a wedding
This early May morn when there is none to wed.

EDWARD THOMAS

As the Team's Head-Brass

As the team's head-brass flashed out on the turn
The lovers disappeared into the wood.
I sat among the boughs of the fallen elm
That strewed the angle of the fallow, and
Watched the plough narrowing a yellow square
Of charlock. Every time the horses turned
Instead of treading me down, the ploughman leaned
Upon the handles to say or ask a word,
About the weather, next about the war.
Scraping the share he faced towards the wood,
And screwed along the furrow till the brass flashed
Once more.
The blizzard felled the elm whose crest
I sat in, by a woodpecker's round hole,
The ploughman said, 'When will they take it away?'
'When the war's over.' So the talk began –

One minute and an interval of ten,

A minute more and the same interval.

'Have you been out?' 'No.' 'And don't want to, perhaps?'

'If I could only come back again, I should.

I could spare an arm, I shouldn't want to lose

A leg. If I should lose my head, why, so,

I should want nothing more ... Have many gone

From here?' 'Yes.' 'Many lost?' 'Yes, a good few.

Only two teams work on the farm this year.

One of my mates is dead. The second day

In France they killed him. It was back in March,

The very night of the blizzard, too. Now if

He had stayed here we should have moved the tree.'

'And I should not have sat here. Everything

Would have been different. For it would have been

Another world.' 'Ay, and a better, though

If we could see all all might seem good.' Then
The lovers came out of the wood again:
The horses started and for the last time
I watched the clods crumble and topple over
After the ploughshare and the stumbling team.

EDWARD THOMAS

This is No Case of Petty Right or Wrong

This is no case of petty right or wrong
That politicians or philosophers
Can judge. I hate not Germans, nor grow hot
With love of Englishmen, to please newspapers.
Beside my hate for one fat patriot
My hatred of the Kaiser is love true: –
A kind of god he is, banging a gong.

But I have not to choose between the two,
Or between justice and injustice. Dinned
With war and argument I read no more
Than in the storm smoking along the wind
Athwart the wood. Two witches' cauldrons roar.
From one the weather shall rise clear and gay;
Out of the other an England beautiful
And like her mother that died yesterday.
Little I know or care if, being dull,
I shall miss something that historians
Can rake out of the ashes when perchance
The phoenix broods serene above their ken.
But with the best and meanest Englishmen
I am one in crying, God save England, lest
We lose what never slaves and cattle blessed.
The ages made her that made us from dust:
She is all we know and live by, and we trust
She is good and must endure, loving her so:
And as we love ourselves we hate her foe.

EDWARD THOMAS

The Answer

O the Tyrant Lord has drawn his sword,
And has flung the scabbard away.
He has said the word that loosed his horde
To ravage, destroy and slay.
'Then where are those who will dare oppose
The blast of my fury's flame?'
But a salty breeze swept across the seas,
And back the clear answer came:
'We have heard the boast of your mighty host,
And slaves will we ne'er become;
Let our deeds declare what our hearts will dare,
We come! We come! We come!'

J.M. LANGSTAFF

A Listening Post

The sun's a red ball in the oak
And all the grass is grey with dew,
Awhile ago a blackbird spoke –
He didn't know the world's askew.

And yonder rifleman and I
Wait here behind the misty trees
To shoot the first man that goes by,
Our rifles ready on our knees.

How could he know that if we fail
The world may lie in chains for years
And England be a bygone tale
And right be wrong, and laughter tears?

Strange that this bird sits there and sings
While we must only sit and plan –
Who are so much the higher things –
The murder of our fellow man ...

But maybe God will cause to be –
Who brought forth sweetness from the strong –
Out of our discords harmony
Sweeter than that bird's song.

ROBERT ERNEST VERNÈDE

The Shell Hole

In the Shell Hole he lies, this German soldier of a year ago;

But he is not as then, accoutred, well, and eager for the foe

He hoped so soon, so utterly, to crush. His muddy skull

Lies near the mangled remnants of his corpse – war's furies thus annul

The pomp and pageantry that were its own. White rigid bones

Gape through the nauseous chaos of his clothes; the cruel stones

Hold fast the letter he was wont to clasp close to his am'rous breast.

Here 'neath the stark, keen stars, where is no peace, no joy, nor any rest,

e lies. There, to the right, his boot, gashed by the great shell's fiendish whim,

Retains – O horrid spectacle! – the fleshless stump that was his limb!

Vile rats and mice, and flies and lice and ghastly things that carrion know

Have made a travesty of Death of him who lived a year ago.

HAMISH MANN

The Soldier

'Tis strange to look on a man that is dead
As he lies in the shell-swept hell
And to think that the poor black battered corpse
Once lived like you and was well.

'Tis stranger far when you come to think
That you may be soon like him ...
And it's Fear that tugs at your trembling soul,
A Fear that is weird and grim!

HAMISH MANN

Tommy's Dwelling

I come from trenches deep in slime,
Soft slime so sweet and yellow,
And rumble down the steps in time
to souse 'some shivering fellow'.

I trickle in and trickle out
Of every nook and corner,
And, rushing like some waterspout,
Make many a rat a mourner.

I gather in from near and far
A thousand brooklets swelling,
And laugh aloud a great 'Ha, ha!'
To flood poor Tommy's dwelling.

HAROLD PARRY

An April Interlude - 1917

April snow agleam in the stubble,

Melting to brown on the new-ploughed fields,

April sunshine, and swift cloud-shadows

Racing to spy what the season yields

Over the hills and far away:

Heigh! And ho! For an April day!

Hoofs on the highroad: *Ride-tr-t-ot!*

Spring's in the wind, and war's forgot,

As we go riding through Picardy.

Up by a wood where a brown hawk hovers,

Down through a village with white-washed walls,

A wooden bridge and a mill-wheel turning,

And a little stream that sports and brawls

Into the valley and far away:

Heigh! and ho! For an April day!
Children and old men stop to stare
At the chattering horsemen from *Angleterre*,
As we go riding through Picardy.

On by the unkempt hedges, budding,
On by the Chateau gates flung wide.
Where is the man who should trim the garden?
Where are the youths of this country-side? –
Over the hills and far away
Is war, red war, this April day.
So for the moment we pay our debt
To the cause on which our faith is set,
As we go riding through Picardy.

Then the hiss of the spurted gravel,
Then the tang of wind on the face,
Then the splash of the hoof-deep puddle,
Spirit of April setting the pace

Over the hills and far away:

Heigh! And ho! For an April day!

Heigh! For a ringing: *Ride-tr-t-ot!*

Ho! – of war we've never a thought

As we go riding through Picardy.

BERNARD FREEMAN TROTTER

A Kiss

She kissed me when she said good-bye –

A child's kiss, neither bold nor shy.

We had met but a few short summer hours;

Talked of the sun, the wind, the flowers,

Sports and people; had rambled through

A casual catchy song or two,

And walked with arms linked to the car
By the light of a single misty star.

(It was war-time, you see, and the streets were dark
Lest the ravishing Hun should find a mark.)

And so we turned to say good-bye;
But somehow or other, I don't know why,

– Perhaps 'twas the feel of the khaki coat
(She'd a brother in Flanders then) that smote

Her heart with a sudden tenderness
Which issued in that swift caress –

Somehow, to her, at any rate
A mere hand-clasp seemed inadequate;

And so she lifted her dewey face
And kissed me – but without a trace

Of passion, – and we said good-bye ...
A child's kiss, ... neither bold nor shy.

My friend, I like you – it seemed to say –
Here's to our meeting again some day!
Some happier day ...
Good-bye.

BERNARD FREEMAN TROTTER

'Ici Repose'

A little cross of weather-silvered wood,

Hung with a garish wreath of tinselled wire,

And on it carved a legend – thus it runs:

'Ici Respose – ' Add what name you will

And multiply by thousands: in the fields,

Along the roads, beneath the trees – one here,

A dozen there, to each its simple tale

Of one more jewel threaded star-like on

The sacrificial rosary of France.

And as I read and read again those words,

Those simple words, they took a mystic sense;

And from the glamour of an alien tongue

They wove insistent music in my brain,
Which, in a twilight hour, when all the guns
Were silent, shaped itself to song.

O happy dead! Who sleep embalmed in glory,
Safe from corruption, purified by fire, –
Ask you our pity? – ours, mud-grimed and gory,
Who still must grimly strive, grimly desire?

You have outrun the reach of our endeavour,
Have flown beyond our most exalted quest, –
Who prate of Faith and Freedom, knowing ever
That all we really fight for's just – a rest,

The rest that only Victory can bring us —
Or Death, which throws us brother-like by you —
The civil commonplace in which 'twill fling us
To neutralize our then too martial hue.

But you have rest from every tribulation
Even in the midst of war; you sleep serene,
Pinnacled on the sorrow of a nation,
In cerements of sacrificial sheen.

Oblivion cannot claim you: our heroic
War-lustred moment, as our youth, will pass
To swell the dusty hoard of Time the Stoic,
That gathers cobwebs in the nether glass.

We shall grow old, and tainted with the rotten

Effluvia of the peace we fought to win,

The bright deeds of our youth will be forgotten,

Effaced by later failure, sloth, or sin;

But you have conquered Time, and sleep forever,

Like gods, with a white halo on your brows –

Your souls our lode-stars, your death-crowned endeavour

That spur that holds the nations to their vows.

BERNARD FREEMAN TROTTER

Evening Clouds

A little flock of clouds go down to rest
In some blue corner off the moon's highway,
With shepherd winds that shook them in the West
To borrowed shapes of earth, in bright array,
Perhaps to weave a rainbow's gay festoons
Around the lonesome isle which Brooke has made
A little England full of lovely noons,
Or dot it with his country's mountain shade.

Ah, little wanderers, when you reach that isle
Tell him, with dripping dew, they have not failed,
What he loved most; for late I roamed a while
Thro' English fields and down her rivers sailed;
And they remember him with beauty caught
From old desires of Oriental Spring
Heard in his heart with singing overwrought;
And still on Purley Common gooseboys sing.

FRANCIS LEDWIDGE

To One Dead

A blackbird singing
On a moss-upholstered stone,
Bluebells swinging,
Shadows wildly blown,
A song in the wood,
A ship on the sea.
The song was for you
And the ship was for me.

A blackbird singing
I hear in my troubled mind,
Bluebells swinging
I see in a distant wind.
But sorrow and silence

Are the wood's threnody,

The silence for you

And the sorrow for me.

FRANCIS LEDWIDGE

The Place

Blossoms as old as May I scatter here,

And a blue wave I lifted from the stream.

It shall not know when winter days are drear

Or March is hoarse with blowing. But a-dream

The laurel boughs shall hold a canopy

Peacefully over it the winter long,

Till all the birds are back from oversea,
And April rainbows win a blackbird's song.

And when the war is over I shall take
My lute a-down to it and sing again
Songs of the whispering things amongst the brake,
And those I love shall know them by their strain.
Their airs shall be the blackbird's song,
Their words shall be all flowers with fresh dews hoar. –
But it is lonely now in winter long,
And, God! to hear the blackbird song once more.

FRANCIS LEDWIDGE

The Unconquered Dead

'... defeated, with great loss.'

Not we the conquered! Not to us the blame
Of them that flee, of them that basely yield;
Nor ours the shout of victory, the fame
Of them that vanquish in a stricken field.

That day of battle in the dusty heat
We lay and heard the bullets swish and sing
Like scythes amid the over-ripened wheat,
And we the harvest of their garnering.

Some yielded, No, not we! Not we, we swear
By these our wounds; this trench upon the hill
Where all the shell-strewn earth is seamed and bare,
Was ours to keep; and lo! we have it still.

We might have yielded, even we, but death
Came for our helper; like a sudden flood
The crashing darkness fell; our painful breath
We drew with gasps amid the choking blood.

The roar fell faint and farther off, and soon
Sank to a foolish humming in our ears,
Like crickets in the long, hot afternoon
Among the wheat fields of the olden years.

Before our eyes a boundless wall of red
Shot through by sudden streaks of jagged pain!
Then a slow-gathering darkness overhead
And rest came on us like a quiet rain.

Not we the conquered! Not to us the shame,
Who hold our earthen ramparts, nor shall cease
To hold them ever; victors we, who came
In that fierce moment to our honoured peace.

JOHN MCCRAE

In Flanders Fields

In Flanders fields the poppies blow
Between the crosses, row on row,
That mark our place; and in the sky
The larks, still bravely singing, fly
Scarce heard amid the guns below.

We are the Dead. Short days ago
We lived, felt dawn, saw sunset glow,
Loved and were loved, and now we lie
In Flanders fields.

Take up our quarrel with the foe:
To you from failing hands we throw
The torch; be yours to hold it high.
If ye break faith with us who die
We shall not sleep, though poppies grow
In Flanders fields.

JOHN MCCRAE

The Anxious Dead

O guns, fall silent till the dead men hear
Above their heads the legions pressing on:
(These fought their fight in time of bitter fear,
And died not knowing how the day had gone.)

O flashing muzzles, pause, and let them see
The coming dawn that streaks the sky afar;
Then let your mighty chorus witness be
To them, and Caesar, that we still make war.

Tell them, O guns, that we have heard their call,
That we have sworn, and will not turn aside,
That we will onward till we win or fall,
That we will keep the faith for which they died.

Bid them be patient, and some day, anon,

They shall feel earth enwrapt in silence deep;

Shall greet, in wonderment, the quiet dawn,

And in content may turn them to their sleep.

JOHN MCCRAE

The Kitchener Chap

He wore twin stripes of gold upon
    An empty tunic sleeve;
His eyes were blue, his face so young
    One hardly could believe
That he had seen the death and hate
That make the whole world grieve.

His hair was fair, his eyes were blue,
    I thought that I could see
(Just when his sunny smile came through)
    The lad he used to be:
Dear happy little mother's lad
    Of only two or three.

But when across his eyes there came

A sudden look of pain –

His mouth set very hard and straight,

He was a man again.

He gave his shattered dreams of youth

That England might remain.

I felt hot tears rise to my eyes

When I looked at the lad;

Brave, gallant, shattered, smiling youth –

He gave us all he had;

For youth so fair, so sorely hurt

All England's heart is sad.

He passed me on a crowded street,

We did not meet again;

He showed me in a sudden flash

Our England's pride and pain.

And when all is long forgot

His memory shall remain.

HORACE BRAY

Marching

(As Seen from the Left File)

My eyes catch ruddy necks
Sturdily pressed back –
All a red brick moving glint.
Like flaming pendulums, hands
Swing across the khaki –
Mustard-coloured khaki –
To the automatic feet.

We husband the ancient glory
In these bared necks and hands.
Not broke is the forge of Mars;
But a subtler brain beats iron
To shoe the hoofs of death
(Who paws dynamic air now).
Blind fingers loose an iron cloud
To rain immortal darkness
On strong eyes.

ISAAC ROSENBERG

Dead Man's Dump

The plunging limbers over the shattered track
Racketed with their rusty freight,
Stuck out like many crowns of thorns,
And the rusty stakes like sceptres old
To stay the flood of brutish men
Upon our brothers dear.

The wheels lurched over sprawled dead
But pained them not, though their bones crunched,
Their shut mouths made no moan.
They lie there huddled, friend and foeman,
Man born of man, and born of woman,
And shells go crying over them
From night till night and now.

Earth has waited for them,
All the time of their growth
Fretting for their decay:

Now she has them at last!
In the strength of their strength
Suspended – stopped and held.

What fierce imaginings their dark souls lit?
Earth! have they gone into you?
Somewhere they must have gone,
And flung on your hard back
Is their souls' sack,
Emptied of God-ancestralled essences.
Who hurled them out? Who hurled?

None saw their spirits' shadow shake the grass,
Or stood aside for the half-used life to pass
Out of those doomed nostrils and the doomed mouth,
When the swift iron burning bee
Drained the wild honey of their youth.

What of us who, flung on the shrieking pyre,

Walk, our usual thoughts untouched,

Our lucky limbs as on ichor fed,

Immortal seeming ever?

Perhaps when the flames beat loud on us,

A fear may choke in our veins

And the startled blood may stop.

The air is loud with death,

The dark air spurts with fire

The explosions ceaseless are.

Timelessly now, some minutes past,

These dead strode time with vigorous life,

Till the shrapnel called 'An end!'

But not to all. In bleeding pangs

Some borne on stretchers dreamed of home,

Dear things, war-blotted from their hearts.

A man's brains splattered on

A stretcher-bearer's face;

His shook shoulders slipped their load,
But when they bent to look again
The drowning soul was sunk too deep
For human tenderness.

They left this dead with the older dead,
Stretched at the cross roads.
Burnt black by strange decay,
Their sinister faces lie;
The lid over each eye,
The grass and coloured clay
More motions have then they,
Joined to the great sunk silences.

Here is one not long dead;
His dark hearing caught our far wheels,
And the choked soul stretched weak hands
To reach the living word the far wheels said,
The blood-dazed intelligence beating for light,
Crying through the suspense of the far torturing wheels

Swift for the end to break,

Or the wheels to break,

Cried as the tide of the world broke over his sight.

Will they come? Will they ever come?

Even as the mixed hoofs of the mules,

The quivering-bellied mules,

And the rushing wheels all mixed

With his tortured upturned sight,

So we crashed round the bend,

We heard his weak scream,

We heard his very last sound,

And our wheels grazed his dead face.

ISAAC ROSENBERG

On Receiving News of the War

Snow is a strange white word;
No ice or frost
Have asked of bud or bird
For Winter's cost.

Yet ice and frost and snow
From earth to sky
This Summer land doth know.
No man knows why.

In all men's hearts it is.
Some spirit old
Hath turned with malign kiss
Our lives to mould.

Red fangs have torn His face.

God's blood is shed.

He mourns from His lone place

His children dead.

O! ancient crimson curse!

Corrode, consume.

Give back this universe

Its pristine bloom.

ISAAC ROSENBERG

Louse Hunting

Nudes – stark and glistening,
Yelling in lurid glee. Grinning faces
And raging limbs
Whirl over the floor one fire.
For a shirt verminously busy
Yon soldier tore from his throat, with oaths
Godhead might shrink at, but not the lice.
And soon the shirt was aflare
Over the candle he'd lit while we lay.

Then we all sprang up and stript
To hunt the verminous brood.
Soon like a demons' pantomime
The place was raging.

See the silhouettes agape,

See the glibbering shadows

Mixed with the battled arms on the wall.

See gargantuan hooked fingers

Pluck in supreme flesh

To smutch supreme littleness.

See the merry limbs in hot Highland fling

Because some wizard vermin

Charmed from the quiet this revel

When our ears were half lulled

By the dark music

Blown from Sleep's trumpet.

ISAAC ROSENBERG

Break of Day in the Trenches

The darkness crumbles away.

It is the same old druid Time as ever,

Only a live thing leaps my hand,

A queer sardonic rat,

As I pull the parapet's poppy

To stick behind my ear.

Droll rat, they would shoot you if they knew

Your cosmopolitan sympathies.

Now you have touched this English hand

You will do the same to a German

Soon, no doubt, if it be your pleasure

To cross the sleeping green between.

It seems you inwardly grin as you pass

Strong eyes, fine limbs, haughty athletes,

Less chanced than you for life,

Bonds to the whims of murder,

Sprawled in the bowels of the earth,

The torn fields of France.

What do you see in our eyes

At the shrieking iron and flame

Hurled through still heavens?

What quaver – what heart aghast?

Poppies whose roots are in man's veins

Drop, and are ever dropping;

But mine in my ear is safe –

Just a little white with the dust.

ISAAC ROSENBERG

Returning, We Hear
the Larks

Sombre the night is.

And though we have our lives, we know

What sinister threat lurks there.

Dragging these anguished limbs, we only know

This poison-blasted track opens on our camp –

On a little safe sleep.

But hark! joy – joy – strange joy.

Lo! heights of night ringing with unseen larks.

Music showering on our upturned list'ning faces.

Death could drop from the dark

As easily as song –

But song only dropped,

Like a blind man's dreams on the sand

By dangerous tides,

Like a girl's dark hair for she dreams no ruin lies there,

Or her kisses where a serpent hides.

ISAAC ROSENBERG

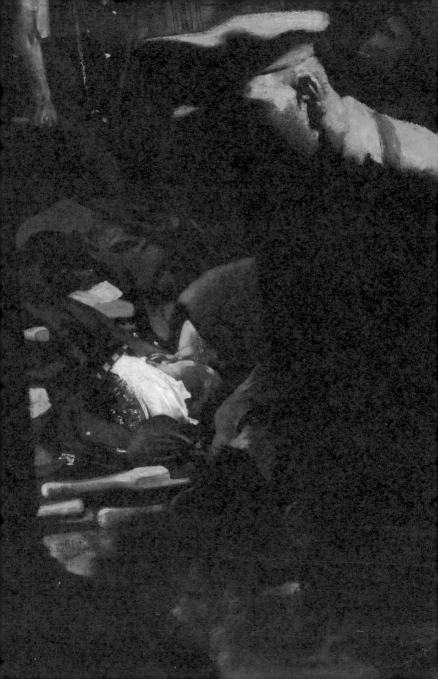

Casualty List

How long, how long
shall there be Something
that can grind the faces of poor men
to an ultimate uniformity of dullness
and grinning trivial meanness?

Or pitchfork them at will
(cheering and singing patriotic doggerel)
to a stinking hell,
noisily, miserably;
till the inevitable comes,
and crushes them
bloodily, meanly?

HENRY LAMONT SIMPSON

Last Song

All my songs are risen and fled away;

(Only the brave birds stay);

All my beautiful songs are broken or fled.

My poor songs could not stay

Among the filth and the weariness and the dead.

There was bloody grime on their light, white feathery wings,

(Hear how the lark still sings),

And their eyes were the eyes of dead men that I knew.

Only a madman sings

When half of his friends lie asleep for the rain and the dew.

The flowers will grow over the bones of my friends;

(The birds' song never ends);

Winter and summer, their fair flesh turns to clay.

Perhaps before all ends
My songs will come again that have fled away.

HENRY LAMONT SIMPSON

Rouge Bouquet

In a wood they call the Rouge Bouquet
There is a new-made grave to-day,
Built by never a spade nor pick
Yet covered with earth ten metres thick.
There lie many fighting men,
Dead in their youthful prime,

Never to laugh nor love again

Nor taste the Summertime.

For Death came flying through the air

And stopped his flight at the dugout stair,

Touched his prey and left them there,

Clay to clay.

He hid their bodies stealthily

In the soil of the land they fought to free

And fled away.

Now over the grave abrupt and clear

Three volleys ring;

And perhaps their brave young spirits hear

The bugle sing:

'Go to sleep

Go to sleep!

Slumber well where the shell screamed and fell.

Let your rifles rest on the muddy floor,

You will not need them any more.

Danger's past;

Now at last,

Go to sleep!'

There is on earth no worthier grave

To hold the bodies of the brave

Than this place of pain and pride

Where they nobly fought and nobly died.

Never fear but in the skies

Saints and angels stand

Smiling with their holy eyes

On this new-come band.

St. Michael's sword darts through the air

And touches the aureole on his hair

As he sees them stand saluting there,

His stalwart sons;

And Patrick, Brigid, Columkill

Rejoice that in veins of warriors still

The Gael's blood runs.

And up to Heaven's doorway floats,

From the wood called Rouge Bouquet,

A delicate cloud of bugle notes

That softly say:

'Farewell!

Farewell!

Comrades true, born anew, peace to you!

Your souls shall be where the heroes are

And your memory shine like the morning-star.

Brave and dear,

Shield us here.

Farewell!'

JOYCE KILMER

Spring Offensive

Halted against the shade of a last hill,
They fed, and lying easy, were at ease
And, finding comfortable chest and knees
Carelessly slept. But many there stood still
To face the stark, blank sky beyond the ridge,
Knowing their feet had come to the end of the world.

Marvelling they stood, and watched the long grass swirled
By the May breeze, murmurous with wasp and midge,
For though the summer oozed into their veins
Like the injected drug for their bodies' pains,
Sharp on their souls hung the imminent line of grass,
Fearfully flashed the sky's mysterious glass.

Hour after hour they ponder in the warm field, –
And the far valley behind, where the buttercups
Had blessed with gold their slow boots coming up,
When even the little brambles would not yield
But clutched and clung to them like sorrowing hands.
They breathe like trees unstirred.

Till like a cold gust thrilled the little word
At which each body and its soul begird
And tighten them for battle. No alarms
Of bugles, no high flags, no clamorous haste, –
Only a lift and flare of eyes that faced
The sun, like a friend with whom their love is done.
O larger shone that smile against the sun, –
Mightier than his whose bounty these have spurned.

So, soon they topped the hill, and raced together

Over an open stretch of herb and heather

Exposed. And instantly the whole sky burned

With fury against them; earth set sudden cups

In thousands for their blood; and the green slope

Chasmed and steepened sheer to infinite space.

Of them who running on that last high place

Leapt to swift unseen bullets, or went up

On the hot blast and fury of hell's upsurge,

Or plunged and fell away past this world's verge,

Some say God caught them even before they fell.

But what say such as from existence' brink

Ventured but drave too swift to sink,

The few who rushed in the body to enter hell,

And there outfiending all its fiends and flames

With superhuman inhumanities,

Long-famous glories, immemorial shames –

And crawling slowly back, have by degrees

Regained cool peaceful air in wonder –

Why speak not they of comrades that went under?

WILFRED OWEN

Mental Cases

Who are these? Why sit they here in twilight?
Wherefore rock they, purgatorial shadows,
Drooping tongues from jaws that slob their relish,
Baring teeth that leer like skulls' teeth wicked?
Stroke on stroke of pain, – but what slow panic,
Gouged these chasms round their fretted sockets?
Ever from their hair and through their hands' palms
Misery swelters. Surely we have perished
Sleeping, and walk hell; but who these hellish?

– These are men whose minds the Dead have ravished.
Memory fingers in their hair of murders,
Multitudinous murders they once witnessed.
Wading sloughs of flesh these helpless wander,
Treading blood from lungs that had loved laughter.

Always they must see these things and hear them,
    Batter of guns and shatter of flying muscles,
    Carnage incomparable, and human squander
    Rucked too thick for these men's extrication.

    Therefore still their eyeballs shrink tormented
    Back into their brains, because on their sense
Sunlight seems a bloodsmear; night comes blood-black;
    Dawn breaks open like a wound that bleeds afresh.
        – Thus their heads wear this hilarious, hideous,
            Awful falseness of set-smiling corpses.
        – Thus their hands are plucking at each other;
        Picking at the rope-knouts of their scourging;
        Snatching after us who smote them, brother,
        Pawing us who dealt them war and madness.

WILFRED OWEN

Disabled

He sat in a wheeled chair, waiting for dark,
And shivered in his ghastly suit of grey,
Legless, sewn short at elbow. Through the park
Voices of boys rang saddening like a hymn,
Voices of play and pleasure after day,
Till gathering sleep had mothered them from him.

About this time Town used to swing so gay
When glow-lamps budded in the light blue trees,
And girls glanced lovelier as the air grew dim,
– In the old times, before he threw away his knees.
Now he will never feel again how slim
Girls' waists are, or how warm their subtle hands.
All of them touch him like some queer disease.

There was an artist silly for his face,
For it was younger than his youth, last year.
Now, he is old; his back will never brace;
He's lost his colour very far from here,
Poured it down shell-holes till the veins ran dry,
And half his lifetime lapsed in the hot race
And leap of purple spurted from his thigh.

One time he liked a bloodsmear down his leg,
After the matches, carried shoulder-high.
It was after football, when he'd drunk a peg,
He thought he'd better join. — He wonders why.
Someone had said he'd look a god in kilts,
That's why; and maybe, too, to please his Meg,
Aye, that was it, to please the giddy jilts
He asked to join. He didn't have to beg;
Smiling they wrote his lie: aged nineteen years.

166

Germans he scarcely thought of; all their guilt
And Austria's, did not move him. And no fears
Of Fear came yet. He thought of jewelled hilts
    For daggers in plaid socks; of smart salutes;
    And care of arms; and leave; and pay arrears;
    Esprit de corps; and hints for young recruits.
And soon, he was drafted out with drums and cheers.

Some cheered him home, but not as crowds cheer Goal.
    Only a solemn man who brought him fruits
    Thanked him; and then enquired about his soul.

Now, he will spend a few sick years in institutes,
    And do what things the rules consider wise,
    And take whatever pity they may dole.
    Tonight he noticed how the women's eyes
Passed from him to the strong men that were whole.
    How cold and late it is! Why don't they come
    And put him into bed? Why don't they come?

WILFRED OWEN

Futility

Move him into the sun –
Gently its touch awoke him once,
At home, whispering of fields unsown.
Always it woke him, even in France,
Until this morning and this snow.
If anything might rouse him now
The kind old sun will know.

Think how it wakes the seeds, –
Woke, once, the clays of a cold star.
Are limbs, so dear-achieved, are sides,
Full-nerved, – still warm, – too hard to stir?
Was it for this the clay grew tall?
– O what made fatuous sunbeams toil
To break earth's sleep at all?

WILFRED OWEN

Smile, Smile, Smile

Head to limp head, the sunk-eyed wounded scanned
Yesterday's *Mail*; the casualties (typed small)
And (large) Vast Booty from our Latest Haul.
Also, they read of Cheap Homes, not yet planned,
For, said the paper, when this war is done
The men's first instincts will be making homes.
Meanwhile their foremost need is aerodromes,
It being certain war has but begun.
Peace would do wrong to our undying dead, –
The sons we offered might regret they died
If we got nothing lasting in their stead.
We must be solidly indemnified.
Though all be worthy Victory which all bought,
We rulers sitting in this ancient spot

Would wrong our very selves if we forgot

The greatest glory will be theirs who fought,

Who kept this nation in integrity.

Nation? – The half-limbed readers did not chafe

But smiled at one another curiously

Like secret men who know their secret safe.

(This is the thing they know and never speak,

That England one by one had fled to France,

Not many elsewhere now, save under France.)

Pictures of these broad smiles appear each week,

And people in whose voice real feeling rings

Say: How they smile! They're happy now, poor things.

WILFRED OWEN

Anthem for Doomed Youth

What passing-bells for these who die as cattle?
    – Only the monstrous anger of the guns.
    Only the stuttering rifles' rapid rattle
    Can patter out their hasty orisons.
No mockeries now for them; no prayers nor bells;
    Nor any voice of mourning save the choirs, –
    The shrill, demented choirs of wailing shells;
    And bugles calling for them from sad shires.

    What candles may be held to speed them all?
    Not in the hands of boys, but in their eyes
    Shall shine the holy glimmers of goodbyes.
    The pallor of girls' brows shall be their pall;
    Their flowers the tenderness of patient minds,
    And each slow dusk a drawing-down of blinds.

WILFRED OWEN

Strange Meeting

It seemed that out of the battle I escaped
Down some profound dull tunnel, long since scooped
Through granites which titanic wars had groined.

Yet also there encumbered sleepers groaned,
Too fast in thought or death to be bestirred.
Then, as I probed them, one sprang up, and stared
With piteous recognition in fixed eyes,
Lifting distressful hands as if to bless.
And by his smile, I knew that sullen hall, –
By his dead smile I knew we stood in Hell.

With a thousand pains that vision's face was grained;
Yet no blood reached there from the upper ground,
And no guns thumped, or down the flues made moan.
'Strange friend,' I said, 'here is no cause to mourn.'

'None,' said the other, 'save the undone years,

   The hopelessness. Whatever hope is yours,

     Was my life also; I went hunting wild

     After the wildest beauty in the world,

   Which lies not calm in eyes, or braided hair;

   But mocks the steady running of the hour,

   And if it grieves, grieves richlier than here.

For by my glee might many men have laughed,

   And of my weeping something has been left,

   Which must die now. I mean the truth untold,

     The pity of war, the pity war distilled.

   Now men will go content with what we spoiled,

     Or, discontent, boil bloody, and be spilled.

   They will be swift with swiftness of the tigress.

None will break ranks, though nations trek from progress.

     Courage was mine, and I had mystery,

Wisdom was mine, and I had mastery:

To miss the march of this retreating world

Into vain citadels that are not walled.

Then, when much blood had clogged their chariot-wheels,

I would go up and wash them from sweet wells,

Even with truths that lie too deep for taint.

I would have poured my spirit without stint

But not through wounds; not on the cess of war.

Foreheads of men have bled where no wounds were.

I am the enemy you killed, my friend.

I knew you in this dark: for so you frowned

Yesterday through me as you jabbed and killed.

I parried; but my hands were loath and cold.

Let us sleep now ...'

WILFRED OWEN

Dulce et Decorum Est

Bent double, like old beggars under sacks,
Knock-kneed, coughing like hags, we cursed through sludge,
Till on the haunting flares we turned our backs
And towards our distant rest began to trudge.
Men marched asleep. Many had lost their boots
But limped on, blood-shod. All went lame; all blind;
Drunk with fatigue; deaf even to the hoots
Of tired, outstripped Five-Nines that dropped behind.

Gas! GAS! Quick, boys! – An ecstasy of fumbling,
Fitting the clumsy helmets just in time;
But someone still was yelling out and stumbling,
And flound'ring like a man in fire or lime ...
Dim, through the misty panes and thick green light,
As under a green sea, I saw him drowning.

In all my dreams, before my helpless sight,
He plunges at me, guttering, choking, drowning.

If in some smothering dreams you too could pace
Behind the wagon that we flung him in,
And watch the white eyes writhing in his face,
His hanging face, like a devil's sick of sin;
If you could hear, at every jolt, the blood
Come gargling from the froth-corrupted lungs,
Obscene as cancer, bitter as the cud
Of vile, incurable sores on innocent tongues, –
My friend, you would not tell with such high zest
To children ardent for some desperate glory,
The old Lie; Dulce et Decorum est
Pro patria mori.

WILFRED OWEN

BIOGRAPHIES

HAROLD BECKH (1894–1916) was born on New Year's Day at Great Amwell, Hertfordshire. He was educated at Cambridge and had intended to become a clergyman. As a second lieutenant he served in trenches near Bertrancourt, France. He was killed by machine-gun fire while on patrol. A collection of his verse, *Swallows in Storm and Sunlight*, was published the following year.

HORACE BRAY (1896–1918) was born in Thamesville, Ontario, and enlisted at the age of 18. A cavalryman, he was seriously wounded at Ypres. He recovered to become a second lieutenant in the Royal Air Force. He was killed in a collision at Shotwick, England.

RUPERT BROOKE (1887–1915) was born in Rugby, Warwickshire. A graduate of King's College, Cambridge, he was a familiar figure in literary and political circles. His first collection of verse, *Poems*, was published in 1911. He entered the war as a sub-lieutenant in the Royal Naval Division, and following his participation in the Antwerp expedition he composed his five war sonnets. While sailing the Aegean on the way to Gallipoli he died of acute blood poisoning, the result of a mosquito bite.

LESLIE COULSON (1889–1916) was born in Kilburn. Before enlisting he was a well-known Fleet Street journalist. He survived being wounded at Gallipoli in 1915, dying at the Battle of the Somme. In 1917 a collection of his poetry, *From an Outpost and Other Poems*, became a bestseller in England.

RICHARD DENNYS (1884–1916) was born in London. Though schooled in medicine, after graduation he pursued a career in the arts. He was mortally wounded at the Battle of the Somme. *There is No Death*, a collection of his poetry, was published the next year.

JULIAN GRENFELL (1888–1915), the eldest son of the Earl of Desborough, was born in London. He was educated at Eton and Oxford and, in 1910, joined the Royal Dragoons. A recipient of the Distinguished Service Order, he was hit by shrapnel during the Second Battle of Ypres. He succumbed to his wounds four weeks later.

W. N. HODGSON (1893–1916), the son of a bishop, was born in Thornbury, Gloucestershire. He volunteered at the beginning of the war and in the following year was sent to France. While there he became a popular writer, describing life in the trenches for readers of *The Saturday Review*, *The Spectator* and other periodicals. He was killed by machine-gun fire near Mametz. A collection of his writing, *Verse and Prose in War and Peace* was published posthumously.

CYRIL HORNE (1887–1916) was born in Scotland and was living in the United States when war was declared. He was killed by a shell while rescuing a wounded soldier near Loos. *Songs of the Shrapnel Shell and Other Verse*, a collection of his writing, was published in 1920.

T.M. KETTLE (1880–1916) was born in Artane, County Dublin. A Member of Parliament, lawyer, professor and journalist, he was an advocate for Irish home rule. He enlisted not long after war was declared and was killed at the Battle of the Somme. In 1917, his wartime writing was collected in the volume *The Ways of War*.

JOYCE KILMER (1886–1918) was born in New Brunswick, New Jersey. After graduating from Columbia University, he found work as an editor, journalist and poet. It was during this time that he wrote 'Trees', his most popular poem. He enlisted in 1917, after the United States entered the war. He was shot by a sniper outside Ourcq, France.

J. M. LANGSTAFF (1883–1917) was born in Richmond Hill, Ontario. A brilliant scholar, he studied law in Toronto. His academic achievements were matched by his military record and he quickly achieved the rank of major. He was killed at the Battle of Vimy Ridge.

FRANCIS LEDWIDGE (1887–1917) was born into an Irish working class family. Though an Irish Nationalist, he volunteered to serve a few months after war was declared. The following year, while serving abroad, his first two collections of verse, *Songs of the Fields* and *Songs of Peace*, were published. He was killed by a shell during the Third Battle of Ypres. *Last Songs*, a third collection of poetry, was published posthumously.

W.S.S. LYON (1886–1915) joined the Royal Scots the year before war broke out. He served in France and Belgium and was killed by shellfire near Ypres.

A collection of verse, *Easter at Ypres 1915 and Other Poems*, was published posthumously.

JOHN McCRAE (1872–1918) was born in Guelph, Ontario. He studied medicine at the University of Toronto, finishing at the top of his class. In 1899, he was awarded a fellowship in pathology at McGill University, but delayed further study to serve in the Boer War. A lieutenant-colonel, he served the greater part of the First World War as a surgeon at the front and at a hospital in Boulogne, where he died of pneumonia complicated by meningitis. His only collection of verse, *In Flanders Fields and Other Poems*, was published a year after his death.

HAMISH MANN was the pseudonym of **ARTHUR JAMES MANN (1896–1917)**. He was born in Broughty Ferry, Forfarshire, and was educated in Edinburgh. A veteran of the Battle of the Somme, he was wounded at Arras and died the following day. A collection of his war poetry, *A Subaltern's Musings*, was published posthumously.

WILFRED OWEN (1893–1918) was born in Ostwestry, Shropshire. Educated at the Birkenhead Institute and the University of London, he was teaching abroad when war broke out. In 1915, he returned to England in order to enlist. In May 1917, while serving in the trenches in France, he was caught in an explosion. Diagnosed with shellshock, he was sent to England in order to recover. He returned to France in August, 1918, and was awarded the Military Cross two months later. On 4 November 1918, he was killed by German machine-gun fire. The first collection of his verse, *Poems* (1920), was edited by his friend and mentor, fellow war poet Siegfried Sassoon.

HAROLD PARRY (1896–1917) was born in Bloxwich. A scholarship student, he was studying at Oxford when war broke out. He was killed by a shell at Ypres. *In Memoriam*, a collection of his poems and letters, was published posthumously.

COLWYN PHILIPPS (1888–1915), the eldest son of the First Baron of St. David's, was born in London. He served as captain in the Royal Horse Guards until his death during the Second Battle of Ypres. A collection of his poetry and prose, *Colwyn Erasmus Arnold Philipps*, was published a few months after his death.

ALEXANDER ROBERTSON (1882–1916) was born in Edinburgh. An academic, he wrote several books, including a biography, *The Life of Robert Moray*. He was killed on the first day of the Battle of the Somme. A collection, *The Last Poems of Alexander Robertson*, was published in 1918.

ISAAC ROSENBERG (1890–1918) was born in Bristol to Russian immigrants. Though a talented poet – his first collection of verse, *Night and Day*, was published in 1912 – he considered himself a portrait artist. He was in South Africa – an attempt to improve his frail health – when war was declared. He returned to England and enlisted and was killed in close combat near the French village of Fampoux. The first posthumous collection of his verse, *Poems*, was published in 1922.

ALAN SEEGER (1888–1916) was born in New York and spent much of his childhood in Mexico. Educated at

Harvard, for several years he lived a bohemian lifestyle in Greenwich Village. He was visiting London, conducting research at the British Museum, when war was declared. He joined the French Foreign Legion and was killed in France at Belloy-en-Santerre. A collection of verse, *Poems*, was published a few months later.

HENRY LAMONT SIMPSON (1897–1918) was born in Crosby-on-Eden, Carlisle. A student at Cambridge, he became a commissioned officer in 1917. He was killed by a sniper at Strazeele, France. His only collection of poetry, *Moods and Tenses*, was published the year after the war ended.

CHARLES HAMILTON SORLEY (1895–1915) was born in Aberdeen, the son of a university professor. After attending Marlborough College he won a scholarship to University College, Oxford, but chose to defer entry to enlist in 1914. Less than a year later he was commissioned as a captain. He was killed by a sniper at the Battle of Loos. A collection of verse, *Marlborough and Other Poems*, was published the year after his death.

R. W. STERLING (1893–1915) was born in Glasgow. The recipient of a scholarship, he was studying at Oxford when war was declared. He was killed at the Second Battle of Ypres, an early casualty of the war. His *Poems* was published by Oxford University Press in 1916.

J.W. STREETS (1885–1917) was born in Whitwell, Derbyshire. At the age of 14, he found work as a coalminer. He enlisted when war was declared and was killed in the Battle of the Somme. A few months later, *The Undying Splendour*, a collection of his verse, was published.

E. WYNDHAM TENNANT (1897–1916) was born in Wiltshire, the son of Baron Glenconnor. His younger brother was Stephen Tennant. As a schoolboy, aged 17, he enlisted at the beginning of the war. He was killed by a sniper's bullet at the Battle of the Somme. His first collection of verse, *Worple Flit and Other Poems*, was published the year of his death.

EDWARD THOMAS (1878–1917) was born in London to Welsh parents. He studied at Oxford on a history scholarship. In 1899, he married the daughter of James Ashcroft Noble, a nineteenth-century literary figure. Encouraged by his father-in-law, he pursued a life in letters as an author, editor and reviewer. His first poems were written in 1914, the year before he enlisted. He was killed by a shell at Arras. Several collections of his verse were published in the years immediately following his death.

BERNARD FREEMAN TROTTER (1890–1917) was born in Toronto and spent much of his youth in Wolfville, Nova Scotia. His initial attempt to enlist thwarted by ill-health, he finally set sail for Europe in March 1916. A little over a year later Trotter was killed by a shell while serving as a Transport Officer at the Front. His only collection of poems, *A Canadian Twilight and other Poems of War and of Peace*, was published the month of the Armistice.

ROBERT ERNEST VERNÈDE (1875–1917) was born in London. A professional writer, prior to the war he had had several books published, including *Fair Dominion*, in which he had recorded his impressions of Canada.

He was killed by machine-gun fire while serving with the Royal Fusiliers. His *War Poems and Other Verses* was published in 1918.

ARTHUR GRAEME WEST (1891–1917) was born in Norfolk and spent his childhood in London. He was educated at Oxford and enlisted as a private in 1915. He quickly rose in ranks to captain before being killed by a sniper outside Bapaume, France. *The Diary of a Dead Officer*, containing extracts from his journal, essays and poems, was published in 1919.

INDEX OF TITLES

1914 I Peace 12

  II Safety 13

  III The Dead 15

  IV The Dead 16

  V The Soldier 17

A Kiss 113

A Listening Post 105

All the Hills and Vales Along 29

An April Interlude – 1917 111

Anthem for Doomed Youth 171

As the Team's Head-Brass 100

Ave, Mater – atque Vale 38

Before Action 43

Better Far to Pass Away

Break of Day in the Trenches 146

'–But a Short Time to Live' 81

Casualty List 151

Champagne, 1914–15 51

Dead Man's Dump 136

Disabled 164

Dulce et Decorum Est 175

Evening Clouds 121

From an Outpost 76

from Dolores 34

Futility 168

God! How I Hate You, You Young Cheerful Men 90

Gone, Gone Again 95

Home Thoughts from Laventie 68

'Ici Repose' 116

I Have a Rendezvous with Death 57

I Tracked a Dead Man Down a Trench 19

In Flanders Fields 129

In Memoriam (Easter, 1915) 95

Into Battle 24

Last Lines 18

Last Song 152

Light After Darkness 66

Lines Before Going   37
Louse Hunting   143
Love of Life   36
Marching   135
Mental Cases   162
On Receiving News of the War   141
Rain   98
Reincarnation   75
Release   22
Release   40
Resurgam   45
Returning, We Hear the Larks   148
Rouge Bouquet   153
Smile, Smile, Smile   169
Spring Offensive   157
Strange Meeting   172
The Aisne, 1914–15   46
The Answer   104
The Anxious Dead   128
The Cherry Trees   99
The Kitchener Chap   131
The Mad Soldier   72
The Night Patrol   87
The Place   123
The Rainbow   78
The Shell Hole   106
The Soldier   108
The Song of Sheffield   63
The Unconquered Dead   125
This is No Case of Petty Right or Wrong   102
To Germany   28
To My Daughter Betty, The Gift of God   65
To One Dead   122
Tommy's Dwelling   110
War   59
When You See Millions of the Mouthless Dead   33
Who Made the Law?   84

INDEX OF FIRST LINES

A blackbird singing   122
A leaping wind from England   40
A little cross of weather-silvered wood   116
A little flock of clouds go down to rest   121
Ah! Hate like this would freeze our human tears   18
All my songs are risen and fled away   152
All the hills and vales along   29
April snow agleam in the stubble   111
As the team's head-brass flashed out on the turn   100
Bent double, like old beggars under sacks   175
Better far to pass away   60
Blossoms as old as May I scatter here   123
Blow out, you bugles, over the rich Dead   15
By all the glories of the day   43
Dear! of all happy in the hour, most blest   13
Exiled afar from youth and happy love   45
God! How I hate you, you young cheerful men   90
Gone, gone again   95
Green gardens in Laventie   68
Halted against the shade of a last hill   157
He sat in a wheeled chair, waiting for dark   164
He wore twin stripes of gold upon   131
Head to limp head, the sunk-eyed wounded scanned   169
How long, how long   151
I come from trenches deep in slime   110
I dropp'd here three weeks ago, yes – I know   72
I have a rendezvous with Death   57
I too remember distant golden days   75
I tracked a dead man down a trench   19
I watch the white dawn gleam   78
If I should die, think only this of me   17
In a wood they call the Rouge Bouquet   153
In Flanders fields the poppies blow   129
In the glad revels, in the happy fetes   51
In the Shell Hole he lies   106
In wiser days, my darling rosebud, blown   65
It seemed that out of the battle I escaped   172
I've tramped South England up and down   76
Move him into the sun   168

My eyes catch ruddy necks   135
Not we the conquered! Not to us the blame   125
Now, God be thanked   12
Nudes – stark and glistening   143
O brother, I have sung no dirge for thee   18
O guns, fall silent till the dead men hear   128
O the Tyrant Lord has drawn his sword   104
Once more the Night   66
Our little hour – how swift it flies   81
Over the top! The wire's thin here, unbarbed   87
Rain, midnight rain, nothing but the wild rain   98
Reach out thy hands, thy spirit's hands, to me   36
She kissed me when she said good-bye   113
Shells, shells, shells   63
Six of us lay in a Dugout   34
Snow is a strange white word   141
Sombre the night is   148
Soon is the night of our faring to regions unknown   37
The cherry trees bend over and are shedding   99
The darkness crumbles away   146
The deathless mother, grey and battle-scarred   38
The flowers left thick at nightfall in the wood   95
The naked earth is warm with spring   24
The plunging limbers over the shattered track   136
The sun's a red ball in the oak   105
There is a healing magic in the night   22
These hearts were woven of human joys and cares   16
This is no case of petty right or wrong   102
'Tis strange to look on a man that is dead   108
To end the dreary day   59
We first saw fire on the tragic slopes   46
What passing-bells for these who die as cattle   171
When you see millions of the mouthless dead   33
Who are these? Why sit they here in twilight   162
Who made the law that men should die in meadows   84
You are blind like us. Your hurt no man designed   28